ELEVATE YOUR LIFE WITH THE POWER OF POSITIVE PERCEPTION

WHAT I NOW KNOW FOR SURE

Vol 1

NKECHI AJAEROH

JUST POSITUDE Co. LLC
INSPIRE THROUGH POSITIVE ACTION

ISBN 978-0-9981040-0-3

Printed in the United States of America.

First Printing 2016

Just Positude Company, LLC

P. O. Box 5394

Williamsburg,

VA, 23188

www.justpositude.com

care@justpositude.com

Social media platforms Facebook, Twitter & Periscope:

@HonestlyKechi

Dedication

To Victor and Victoria Ajaeroh my beautiful parents who are no longer here with us. To the love, light and laughter you left.

Rest on.

Table of Contents

Preface

In this invigorating and uplifting self-improvement book, Elevate Your Life with the Power of Positive Perception: What I Now Know For Sure, this badass army reservist, military wife, writer, speaker, and mom takes you on the journey of finding freedom, fulfillment and new meaning in the things around you. She explains how positive perception can lead to personal elevation, personal growth and personal bliss. Her light-heartedness and sense of humor shines through as she shares inspiring stories, life lessons and fun exercises throughout the ten chapters of this book. The exercises and stories in this book will help you understand the power of your thoughts. You will learn ways to uplift and enrich your life so that you can successfully reach your goals.

This book will encourage, inspire and motivate you to take action towards your next goal, whether it's big or small. As you read this great book, you will understand the need to focus on the things that will serve you and build you up. You will feel empowered to improve your life and circumstances with the power of positive perception. Chapters such as "One Life to Live" and "Tomorrow is Not Promised" help you understand that you only have one shot at this incredible thing called "life;" and you have to make it fantastic, "fun-tastic", sensational and worth the ride for you. Another chapter, "The Mind is very Powerful," reminds the reader about the power of the mind. It explains why the mind is in fact a super power, an originator of dreams, ideas and visions, an incubator and much more. It also explores how your mind can set you free.

Another outstanding feature of this book is its simplicity. It shows how general knowledge, or things you may have known before, can impact you differently and have new meanings in your life. The bottom line is that by the time you are done with this book, you will experience what I call the #PowerOfPositive PerceptionEffect or #POPPEffect. You will know how to focus on the things that will serve you. You will take charge of your life and go after your goals and dreams because the time for elevation is NOW.

For more information, please contact the author Nkechi Ajaeroh here:

www.justpositude.com or www.afriscopetv.com

www.twitter.com/HonestlyKechi

www.periscope.tv/HonestlyKechi

www.facebook.com/HonestlyKechi

Email: honestlykechi@gmail.com

Introduction

Knowledge is one very powerful thing that we can trade in for everything. In my opinion, knowledge is the wisdom, to use what you know to access what you don't. It helps you to realize the power and value of the things you do not know. In other words, knowledge can be a guiding wisdom, a light and a mental balance only if you let it. As an individual whenever you confidently tap into the reserve of what you know, you will start to become better because you now know better. It is often said that *knowledge is power,* and I have always believed it to be so and still do. However, in recent years people, individuals and even groups have begun to say that *applied knowledge is truly where the power belongs.* That is applying the knowledge you have to solve problems you encounter. In other words if I know and I didn't apply, it doesn't count, or does it? Let's use the stop sign as an example. You know that a red light means stop. Then one afternoon you are in a hurry to get somewhere. And even though you see that the light is red, you don't stop and keep going anyway. At that moment in time your knowledge of the red light and its consequences did not empower you. And then, you receive the traffic violation in the mail. And perhaps you decide to go to the court to fight it. What will your defense be? Are you going to tell the judge you were in a hurry, or that you forgot? Or you thought the light was still yellow and it quickly turned red. Unfortunately, I doubt if any of these excuses will work because ignorance of the law doesn't save you from the wrath of the law. Knowledge is supposed to help us make informed decisions. I think it is right to say that knowledge has the power to make us great. On the other hand, if what you know is not helping you get a handle on things, then it becomes necessary to evaluate what you know or think you know in order to get the full benefits.

As I desired to serve more, give more and appreciate more, I began the journey of wanting to fully live in my calling, my legacy and my purpose. I started to realize there are a couple of things that stand out differently for me right now. Day after day, I continue to appreciate the opportunity of perceiving things positively. I mean seeing old situations in a different light. This new direction of thinking and understanding is starting to empower me, enlighten me and inspire me. And now, I strongly feel the urge to share it with you because I know for certain that the power of positive perception will change your life just like it did mine. The Bible states that when we are kids we think like children. But as we begin to grow and mature, we begin to think like adults and become fully aware of our decisions. Sometimes in life the difference between living in your greatness and merely existing can be understanding the difference between the two. Or simply applying what you already know in another way. In any case, I personally believe that it is imperative to positively perceive the circumstances around you in order to create, elevate and grow. With all the negativity going on in the world today, it becomes even more important to see the good in every situation.

I still remember vividly downloading the Periscope application, and appreciating the possibilities of this new app. With Periscope, you can see people from all over the world sharing fascinating stories, messages and more. I still remember thinking and telling myself, "Oh no, I will never be able to do that." I still remember signing up to use Periscope with my Twitter account in August 2015 and joining my amazing #Peri10k community that same day. I still refused to broadcast but showed up every single day to support the rest of the team. I then remember eventually taking a leap of faith to broadcast after several weeks. It took close to a month and then I mustered up some courage by telling myself, "You know you can do it." And then, I did it - my first broadcast. It still feels like yesterday but it happened in September 2015. It was serene. It was magnificent. It was unbelievable. It was an undeniable example of the power of positive perception. My entire life changed the moment I started to see things differently. Today I have my own periscope community #Afriscopetv where we support people of African descent on Periscope and beyond. I still can't believe how much I have grown and how much difference a year makes. Instead of seeing the walls and ceilings that could hinder me from using Periscope or anything in life, I began to see light and open doors of opportunity at the end of the tunnel. This book is a testimony to the great quote by our beloved Wayne Dyer that says, "When you change how you look at things, the things you look at will change."

1

WE HAVE JUST ONE LIFE TO LIVE

One Big Miracle

Growing up in Africa gave me an opportunity to appreciate more than anything this life and freedom that I enjoy today. I wouldn't say growing up there was entirely hard, but it was interesting. And it is still the same for many people in most developing countries even in this day and age as I pen this note. Despite the physical hardship such as a lack of readily affordable drinking water, electricity, and public transportation during those childhood years, I still have fond memories of my mother's kindness and giving spirit, my fathers' presence and my friends' silliness and good humor. Unarguably, life is one big miracle wrapped up in a journey. But do you know and believe this for sure, that is, for a fact? And if you do believe, are you enjoying this big miracle to the fullest? I will truthfully tell you that I didn't always believe. I use to think that we have more than *one* lifetime. But thanks to the almighty God for making me realize now rather than later about the awesomeness of this one amazing adventure.

Fortunately, through all I have seen and been through, one thing that I have come to know for certain is that there is more to life than just existing. And even though you and I have *one life to live*, we can make the best use of it only if we believe in the miracle of life. Now more than ever I know for certain that life in its entirety is a miracle. This realization was a huge light bulb moment for me. And I vow to be more respectful of this beautiful life that I am given. I vow to accomplish the goals that I really want and try my hand at many things especially the ones that will bring me joy, peace of mind and fulfillment. Now, I do know for sure that Life is precious. Life is light. Life is hope. Life is purpose. Life is mission. Life is vision. Life is accomplishments. Life is success even when we fail trying. Life is a dream. Life is beautiful. Life is a blessing. Life is a miracle. Life is a journey. Most importantly life is everything you want it to be!

Nick Vujicic

I want to share with you an incredible story of life, strength, willpower and conquering adversity. I consider the story of Nick Vujicic to be a tale of life. It shows our capabilities towards the challenges of life and the indomitable will of the human spirit. This powerful testimony attests to the power of positive perception in this journey of life. In fact, I consider his story to be one of the blessings of my lifetime, which truly changed my life for the better. This is the story of Nicholas James "Nick" Vujicic, an Australian Christian Evangelist and motivational speaker born without limbs. As a child, Nick had challenges fitting in because he wasn't like the other kids. He was bullied and yet he survived it. He went to college and graduated with double majors in accounting and finance. He founded a non-profit called "Life Without Limbs" and a speaking company "Attitude is Altitude." He travels the world speaking encouragement and hope to people of all nations. People are truly changing and taking the next actionable step after hearing his story. He has been able to create an amazing life despite what can be considered a misfortune. Nick knows we all have only *one shot at life*. His circumstances never stopped him. And his thoughts of what he couldn't accomplish never stopped him. Instead, Nick focused on what he could do with what he had.

What can we learn from this man? How can you and me possibly go forward without been held back by our past, our present and our future thoughts. What are you doing today to get you where you want to be tomorrow? How are you living your life today, not tomorrow, because you don't know what tomorrow is going to bring. Start now! Start today! Waiting for the right time is wasting the now time. It is unbelievable how this young man is living the best possible life from what he has at the moment and even helping people with limbs do that too. How amazing is that? He is not sitting down and waiting until his miracles happen, or until his hands and legs appear before he starts living. He is going out there changing life from his story and what he has been through. What is your excuse? Why are you not living? Please tell yourself that enough is enough. Make a decision to take back your life today!

Watch out for Destiny Destroyers and This Miracle Is Broken

I have seen destinies hijacked, dreams stolen, and successes cut short because of a lack of knowledge and inability to meticulously apply it. In some societies history has revealed that some lives were said to be more valuable than others. For instance, in some traditional African societies, the king's life is considered superior to those of his subjects. My mother told me that years ago when she was still a little girl growing up in the village, there were some communities that practice a dreadful tradition. Whenever a king dies, he will be buried with someone that is alive. I mean another human being. At that time it was a tradition that a king should not be buried alone. A king is very important, seen as God by some, and even at death valued more than a precious life? When I first heard the story I couldn't quite understand it. But the truth is that you have to watch out for destiny destroyers, stealers and killers in this life - even right now. If you do not make a decision about how you want your life to go, others will make it for you. The belief that a king needs company in the grave was beyond me. And this unfortunate person is buried alive next to the King. His life was cut short. His dream died with him and he never had the opportunity to become what he was created to be. I wondered and pondered upon this piece of history and I became really uneasy. At this time, it felt as if people think that some individuals are created to serve as an emissary to others.

But today, I want you to know that you are created for your own purpose and greatness. And you will live to fulfill that destiny and mission. We all are created by the almighty God, the ultimate creator himself. And we are all created in His image, therefore we are equal before him! And NO, this tradition is no longer in existence today. Thank goodness! However, unfortunately, some of us haven't learned from stories like this one. People are still living lackadaisically, allowing others to hijack their destiny and cut short their dreams and miracles. Please don't be one of those individuals. Today, stop living like a cat with nine lives. Start living your amazingly awesome life as a miracle.

Finding My Purpose

What if I don't know what this life has in store for me? What if I haven't fully realized what my purpose, mission, or destiny is? What I am supposed to be or do? Are you still wondering and questioning what your life mission is? Well, asking yourself the above questions and being sincere with your answers is a great way to start in order to fully understand what you are on this earth to accomplish. Another idea is to take an inventory of your day. Ask yourself, "Is what I am doing everyday leading to an accomplishment of a particular goal?" What do you want to see happen in your life in the next month, next three months or nine months? What would you want to accomplish in the next two, five or ten years? Are you intentionally working towards those things? If your answer is no, then you need to become very conscious and intentional about how you spend your day going forward. You have to take back control of your life. In order to live a life of purpose, you need visions, goals and actionable steps. You have to control what happens in the times of your day. If not, your day will dictate what happens to you.

Another way to find your purpose is to appreciate what you have and where you are. Gratitude is deep, powerful and profound. Gratitude sets the tone for everything else to thrive on. Gratitude is the foundation to make our dreams come true. And I had this realization on my own epic journey. Before I used to complain a lot and blame the circumstances that weren't going very well in my life at that time. However, appreciating whatever is going on with you right now will give you hope for greater blessings to come. Perhaps, the Lord will bless the seed you have in your hand now or open an entirely new door, but you have to take a step. And you do that by appreciating where you are and working hard for more.

If you really understand that you have one shot at life, then feel very free to give yourself the permission and freedom to dream, to visualize, and to have goals that will both excite and scare you. Remember, to live a life of purpose, there is no other choice out there than to push beyond your comfort zone, your physical pain, your excuses and even some seemingly logical thoughts.

I took the inventory of my life and appreciated all the blessings in my life, some of which were seen before as obstacles. And now I can say that I am so grateful for this life and hopeful for an opportunity to make a formidable impact in my generation and the generations after me. In fact, you are reading this book because of my realization that *I have just one life and I want to make it count.* And I have a willingness to do more for myself and for others around me. This new perception is requiring me to give my best possible shot at everything now. And I know it will do the same for you too!

I am certain that the power of positive perception will empower you to view this life, your miracle from a different angle - an angle that will serve you better. Remember, it is important how we view what we see. What are you seeing right now? How are you seeing it? The ultimate thing for you to know today from this chapter is that you have *only one life to live,* and you choose how you want to live it. I encourage you to begin to live with the knowledge of what you have heard today. Your desire should be to live in your greatness and purpose without doubt and question! And there is no better time to start than now. See you at the top my friend.

Chapter 1 Assignments:

Tip: get a pen and your journal or paper if no journal.

Affirmations to help you begin today. Be certain to say and believe these sentences. Or better still; please feel free to write out your own affirmations according to how you feel and what you see.

a) My life is beautiful and blessed, I will not believe otherwise regardless of the circumstances around me.

b) I will be more mindful of what I do, and engage in consistent positive actions because I have this precious life today.

c) I will live my life to the fullest and enjoy the blessings that God and the universe throws at me.

1. Take 10-20 minutes for a reflection about life and where you are on your journey.

2. Write down how you feel about life at this stage. For example, are you happy, sad, blessed, or excited?

3. Allow yourself to dream. Write down the visions you see for yourself. For example, what do you want to be in the future? Business owner? Motivational speaker? Author? Coach? Fashion designer, etc.?

4. Today, decide about where you want your future to go. Knowing is the first step.

Notes

_____

_____

_____

_____

_____

_____

_____

_____

_____

_____

_____

_____

_____

_____

_____

_____

_____

_____

_____

_____

2

Tomorrow Is Not Promised

Re-Understand Your Now

You probably have heard the phrase, "tomorrow is not promised," over and over again. I have myself so this is not a new phrase, not all. What is new for me, however, is the understanding of it or rather the re-understanding of it. My new perception and comprehension of this phrase is helping me chart a new course for my life. I will honestly tell you that I now truly get it for sure. And I absolutely understand that *tomorrow is not promised*, especially with the passing of my mother in January 2013. I realized that the next second, minute or day is never promised. There is no reason to live like it's promised, not anymore. There is no reason not to capitalize on what you have right now, because what you have at this moment is what you can lay claim to. What you have at this moment is more precious than silver, gold or diamonds. What you have at this moment is your gift - the gift of life because you are alive, breathing. The Bible says your gift will make a way for you (Proverbs 18:16). Your gift will provide for you. Your gift will put food on the table for you. This means that you have everything you need right now. You may not feel that way, but you do. And I urge you to begin to operate with that authority, understanding and power. Be brave to use your gift today not tomorrow. For tomorrow, my dear, is not promised.

Yes, sometimes, situations get rough and scratchy. And if care is not taken, you can lose sight of who you really are. You could begin to believe the lies around you - the little mean voices and the naysayers. But today, I want to encourage you to stay solid, and remind you that your gift is waiting for your greatness. What are you going to create today? Don't wait until tomorrow. Remember, as the child of the almighty Father you have everything you need at this time to begin your mission. The work you put in today will decide what kind of life you will enjoy tomorrow. How well you use what you have today seriously impacts how your tomorrow will be. The time is now to allow your gift to grow, glow and shine. You can no longer put your gifts into hiding and wait for an unending *tomorrow*. Let your gift make a way for you. As Mahatma Gandhi said, and I love this quote so very much, "Live as if you were to die tomorrow. Learn as if you were to live forever."

Wake Up

For everyone breathing and walking around on this planet earth, there comes a time when you decide that you're done and you want better things in your life, right? For some people it's a realization that the things they have been doing is no longer serving them. For others, it could be a wake up call like getting fired from a job, going bankrupt or a misfortune. A wake up could also mean ditching those excuses, which may be genuine and going all in for what you now believe and/or want. Unfortunately, there are people out there that may never wake up. There are others who will continue to endure until the very end. That is not who I want to be, and I know that is not who you want to be either. It's important that you wake up to your dreams. It's important that you wake up to your purpose. It's important that you quit sitting on the fence and take a side. Begin to take action on your side today. Remember, *tomorrow is not promised.* Never ever has been, never will be.

You cannot entirely figure everything out before you start because *clarity comes by engagement* according personal development experts. However, sometimes as humans, we are tempted to do so. And, I am not by any means downplaying the role of research, planning and mapping out your route. Of course it is good to research, plan and prepare instead of rushing into an action. But then, it will also be completely unwarranted for you to spend all your time researching and planning without taking actionable steps. There is no reason to keep sleeping in the daytime and well past bedtime. Hello! When you realize that tomorrow is not promised, it becomes even more imperative that you wake up from your slumber. And you must stay sober, informed and alert. There is no better time than now because now is what you have. Finally, resolve to keep trying until you hit your goal. Be prepared to be in it for the long haul. Do not give up. Start now. Start today. Keep going until you see a desired result.

The Urgency of Now

The story of Kentucky Fried Chicken (KFC) founder, Colonel Sanders, is an amazing story. I love his journey, his persistence and his tenacity. This man worked hard like most of us and retired like any other person. Then, when he received his first social security check, he realized that "Oh, this money is darn too small, and I don't want to spend my retirement years like this!" This occurrence woke him up instantly and he made a decision. He didn't stay in the situation to wallow in complaints or maybe wait for the appropriate time. But right there, he woke up to the realities around him and took a giant step that impacted the world and continues to impact the whole world positively. Remember, any age is a great age to wake up and claim the things that rightly belong to you. Do not say you are too old to start or even too young. Colonel Sanders started when he was well over 50 years. Any day is a great day to start. All you need to do is be willing to take back your power, your freedom, and your life.

Stay Up

Before I proceed I am going to tell you what "staying up" is not. Staying up is not waking up from sleep in the middle of the night and deciding, "Oh, I don't want to go back to sleep anymore." Staying up is not waking up abruptly from your mid-afternoon nap and couldn't go back to sleep because you are just not the kind of person that falls asleep easily. Staying up is not when you couldn't sleep all night because your baby was fussy, cranky and inconsolable. Nope! That's not what I am talking about here. Staying up is when you decide to stay alert, intentional and conscious of how you spend your minutes, hours and days because you now have a clear and particular goal or purpose in mind that you want to pursue. You make the ultimate decision and totally resolve that you are going to start living in that purpose and greatness. This purpose now becomes your driving force, your power, your motivation, your dynamism and your energy.

Even though you may still need to stay up in the middle of the night to work towards this goal, the truth of the matter is that you now know what you want. You now know what you are pursuing. You now know your purpose. And you are no longer letting your life tick away by luck. Rather, you are living by the intentions of your purpose. So, when you realize that *tomorrow is not promised*, it now becomes imperative to stay up each moment to live your legacy so you can leave a great legacy.

Waking up is one thing. Staying up is another thing. Just like sleep itself, sometimes someone can get up and fall right back into it. Nonetheless, my prayer is to stay up to deal with the work that I need to tackle. After realizing how much time I wasted without pursuing my dreams, goals, and purpose, I woke up and made a decision to reclaim my life. That is, I made a strong-willed decision to keep my eyes open - not literally.

Experts say that waking up is somewhat easier than staying up, because you will need some willpower to stay up. You are going to need self-discipline, dedication, determination and perseverance to stay up even when you are tired and worn-out. You will still have to maintain those principles that will keep you awake. You may also need to burn some late night oils to stay up. As for me, I truly wanted to become an education advocate for girls and a writer, so I became determined to start. And as I write this piece, I see everything beginning to fall in place and unfold naturally. This is where I am supposed to be at this time. Since starting on this journey a couple of concepts have enabled me to stay up. Please allow me to share them with you.

Number one, be willing and ready to stretch your mind. Put differently, be open to new ideas and knowledge. Remodel or readjust your old views and understanding if you want to move up in life. Also be ready to challenge the old negative thoughts that have held you back. As you learn, you will become better equipped and more prepared to oppose, dispute and defy all those beliefs that have stopped you for so long. Learning is one of the things I now enjoy more than anything else. I personally think that knowledge and learning are very important in life and even more important when you start pursuing your purpose. They help you to fully see and appreciate the beauty around your journey irrespective of what circumstances and situations say.

Number two, start associating yourself with the best. According to self-improvement guru, Jim Rohn, you are a product of the five people you spend most of your time with. To be honest, I didn't know this before but I am glad I know now. For anyone to move more fully into their purpose, they are going to have to stay up and work for it. And this includes equipping yourself with the necessary tools including humans. So, if the old friends you have are no longer serving you, maybe it's time to let go. Begin to surround yourself with people that will build you up. Decide to only spend time with the people that will lift you up and will not be afraid to tell you the truth. These people are the kind you need at this time. When particular knowledge is no longer serving you, it could be for three main reasons. First, the knowledge has run its course, and its outdated, expired and dead. Second, your situation has expired and you are no longer in need of that knowledge. So, listening to it will be a total disservice and waste of time to you. Third, that very knowledge was never applied or used so it became empty. And now you will need to update, revamp or renew it before it can function properly.

This understanding can also be applicable to the people in our lives. Have the people in your life become outdated? Do they still serve you? Are they still relevant to where you are going at this time? Again, only you can answer this question. And I urge you to answer truthfully. If the answer is "NO," then it maybe time to look elsewhere. These outdated relationships may not be able to help you stay up, or hold you up when you begin to fall asleep again.

Show Up Prepared

Woody Allen once said that, "Eighty percent of success is showing up." But I want to add that you must *show up prepared and willing to do your best.* In most cases, what you give out to the universe is what you get back. This is karma. Even in our own private or personal lives, showing up consistently is very important. For instance, if you are a college student, it would be very important that you go to school every day, attend classes and complete related assignments. You can't say, "Oh no, I will only show up to class on quiz day or exam day." Your success on the quizzes and exams would be a result of the work you have put in before that time. In other words, if you were never consistent with going to class, doing your assignments and studying, then you may not do very well on the exam. It is as simple as that. There is a saying that defines success as "preparedness meeting opportunity." Thus, it is really important that we prepare before opportunity knocks on the door.

Actor Samuel L. Jackson is a prime example of what I mean by showing up prepared. This man started acting in 1972. *Together For Days* was his debut film, but he did not get his big break until he played *Jules* in the 1993 classic *Pulp Fiction.* Before this big role that happens to have been written for him by director *Quentin Tarantino* he still showed up to movie sets and stages for all the smaller roles. He personally wanted to succeed and he prepared himself for that success. Who knew he was in the movie *Coming to America*? Who knew he worked as a stand in for *The Cosby Show* for Bill Cosby for three years. You cannot fold your hands and say, "I will sit and wait right here until opportunity knocks on my door. Then I will start preparing." This response will amount to you setting yourself up for failure. "If you fail to plan you plan to fail," as the famous quote says. Success does not happen by luck, chance or accident. Intentional and consistent preparation lays the groundwork for success. This simply means that you as an individual have to ultimately decide what success means to you and how successful you want to be. And then, you put in the work. Remember, planning and preparing ahead of time is actually very important in anything you do in life because it shows that you are ready for the next level.

So, one thing I now know for sure as I conclude this chapter is that tomorrow is not promised. And when you realize this to be true, what do you do? Number one, you wake up. Number two, you find everything within your willpower to stay up. And number three, you begin to show up prepared and ready to offer your best ever to the world today. See you at the top my friend.

Chapter 2 Assignments:

Tip: get a pen and your journal or paper if no journal.

1. Write down where you are at this moment in time. Some examples include 9-5 job worker, business owner, aspiring fashion designer, fashion blogger, aspiring blogger, online biz owner, etc.

   Another tip: Remember to always think big and start small.

2. Write down what you want to see happen in your life in the next six months.

3. Write down what you are going to wake up from. Some possibilities include TV watching time, bad relationships, energy-sucking friends, etc.

4. Write down monthly goals towards your six months goal.

5. Write down 3 ways you are going to stay up. Then, write down 3 ways to keep yourself accountable.

6. Write down 3 daily action steps to prepare you for this goal.

Notes

_____

_____

_____

_____

_____

_____

_____

_____

_____

_____

_____

_____

_____

_____

_____

_____

_____

_____

_____

_____

3

Set the Tone for Your Life

Step up and the World Will Catch up

I never knew that I could confidently set the tone for my life, for my decisions, for my visions until I read the story of Rosa Parks during the February 2016 Black History Month. As we celebrated the historic observance on Periscope a lot of things begin to manifest for me. And boom, like a light bulb yet again, I realize for sure that I am the writer of my own story. I am the chief operator of my bus. I am the main character in my play. I am the dreamer of my dreams. I am the words that I speak to myself. I am everything that I want to be and more. And I have the paper and the pen to write whatsoever I wish in my story, as my story. Then I asked myself, "What are you writing into your book and into your life." At that time, I realized that I have the *yam and the knife* as Ibos of Nigeria would say. And I can cut any piece I desire for consumption. This is such a blessing.

Setting the tone for your life means a lot of things, such as setting your pace, your rhythm and your rate. It will enable you to make productive and favorable decisions. Guess what, if you start walking faster, people that really want to walk with you will catch up. So, instead of slowing down for people to catch up with you, pick up your tempo and the people that really care about you will catch up. So is life. Remember Rosa Parks? By the time she bluntly refused to give up her seat and stood up for what she believed to be the truth, the society started catching up with her. Her single act of bravery tripled the ripple effect that affected the entire society, the entire continent, and the entire world. And today, men and women, Black and White, Jews and Gentiles, have all continued to ride the bus, train and other transportations safely without major discrimination.

Set the Tone on How You Treat Yourself

Love, Accept and Appreciate YOU

I have seen situations whereby individuals treat themselves according to other people's opinion of them. Please, whatever you do, never ever allow people to dictate how your life should go.

Always remember that your life's decisions are yours and only yours to make. By the time you are allowing people's opinions of you to set the tone in your life, then you are losing the grip on your own life and losing sight of what is most important: YOU! The best and first way to begin setting the tone for how you treat yourself is by loving yourself. Self-love and acceptance is highly important because it sets the foundation for everything else to follow. The truth is that you cannot give what you do not have. This is contrary to what is actually seen in society today because everything starts from you. Loving, accepting and appreciating yourself will empower you to understand you are worth more irrespective of your present or future situation. Loving yourself also puts you in the right frame of mind to be able to give the same love, acceptance and appreciation to other people.

I know you would agree with me that the person who never works out or goes to the gym will be unlikely to encourage other people to do the same, right? But when you as a person value the importance of going to the gym, working out or staying fit, then you are likely to encourage the people around you to do the same. This is equally true with everything else in life. Perhaps you have seen someone, or know someone, that never summoned the courage to pursue his dream and aspiration. Those are the kind of people that will likely discourage others as well. I remember a person like that in my life. It is not that they don't want you to succeed. The fact is that they are projecting their fears onto you. So, even if you are not able to get anything done today, close your eyes and realize how beautiful or handsome you are. Accept yourself the way you are. Begin to appreciate all that you are; such as a great person, loving and caring heart, a helper, an "accomplisher" an encourager, a builder, and a giver. Appreciate everything that you are and equally everything that you have forgotten that you are. Love on yourself like no other. Please go ahead and do it!

Be Accountable: Keep Promises to Yourself

Most often we strive to do our best in most situations we find ourselves. We try to perform well and deliver on promises, contracts, etc. (to others), but sometimes we fail repeatedly to fulfill the promises we make to ourselves. For instance, we say that we want to lose 40 pounds. And we tell ourselves that beginning tomorrow we are going start eating right (more greens, more water, less fried and less fast food), exercising and going to the gym. Then we start. The first day went well, and so did the second and third day. By the fourth day, we begin to slip back into our old ways and saying, "Oh, I have headache. I can't exercise today. I will start again tomorrow." "Oh I don't have time to cook some food. I will just grab this quick burger and fries from this fast food place and make some food tomorrow." And just like that you start going back to your old ways without making the necessary changes you intended to make.

One of the ways you set the tone for how you treat yourself is by fulfilling promises to yourself. Do what you say you are going to do for you. Deliver on your promises to yourself, just like you would on other peoples' promises and contracts. I can't stress more the importance of deciding to become accountable to yourself. When you promise yourself to go to the gym three times a week - do it. When you promise yourself that from today forward, you will eat more homemade meals, then make time to cook and do it. When you promise yourself that you are going to start writing your book, and you want to write 500 words every day for the next 20 days - do it. Fulfilling promises to yourself is the only way you can break free from those old circles and begin to set a new tone and pace for your life to go.

Forgiveness Is Powerful. Forgive Yourself

Forgiveness strengthens. Forgiveness is kindness. Forgiveness is beautiful. Forgiveness is acceptance. And most importantly, forgiveness is love. When you forgive, you let go of the powers that are holding you back. You begin to accept the open doors and windows of blessings to your future. Forgiveness enables healing. Without authentic forgiveness it may be difficult for you to completely trust yourself and others. Forgiveness is one of the simplest, yet most powerful ways, to set the tone for your life. Because when you forgive, you are no longer allowing yourself to be held bound by the weight of your struggle, the heaviness of your hurt, the sadness of your story, your yesterdays or yester-years. Rather, you are in a place of peace and love, a place of creation, a place of connection and a place of possibility.

Most times when we talk about forgiveness, our minds can quickly go towards the people that hurt us. We seem to forget about ourselves. What about the blame you pile on yourself when you fail to make the cut? Yes, it is paramount and absolutely important that you forgive people that hurt or wronged you. However, it is also important, if not more important, that you forgive yourself from the guilt and hurt you have been carrying for a very long time or even from last night. You probably don't have a serious crime or a load of guilt that you may need to forgive yourself for or heal yourself from, which is amazing. What about those "I should have, I would have, I could have" moments. Those thoughts are still some of the things that hold you back. In setting the tone for your life and how you treat yourself, you really need to let go. You need to say bye-bye to that old wound and embrace your new future, this awesomeness, with a beautiful smile and a heart of gold. I pray that as you read this book, the power of forgiveness will find its way through your heart. I pray that you will begin to set yourself free and set a tone for your life, in Jesus' name, Amen. Remember, only you have the power to forgive yourself, so go do it. NOW!

Set the Tone on How Others Treat You

Human Interaction: A Necessity

One beautiful thing about life is the beauty of seeing and interacting with other people. Every day we meet people for many reasons. For instance, when we enter an office to transact business, or even in the subway, park, mall and in many other places, we meet people. And if you are a student you even meet more and more people. So, every blessed day, we all have reason to meet new people and run into old ones. Sometimes, people stay in our lives longer, other times shorter. There are also people who are in our lives from the day we came into this beautiful world, and they have never left our side. They are there through thick and thin. They are a part of us because we did not choose them. And they did not choose us. However, somehow we found ourselves in the same fold, the same affinity, the same kinship, and here we are, one family.

Destiny and God put us in our different respective families, which I think is so amazing. How awesome that the creator knows where we are supposed to be and he manifests that for us. We are in our families for life, forever and for the longest run. So, as human beings, human interaction is a must. I have never seen a reclusive person from birth through adulthood. This is why it becomes highly imperative that you set the tone for how you would want to be treated by other people, including family members. We must always lead the way for our lives and for everything else under our control. We can't live our lives on luck saying, "Oh, I hope I am lucky and he wouldn't ask me to do A, B & C." Well, say no!

Don't Accept What You Don't Want

One of the ways to set the tone for how other people treat you is by not accepting what you do not want. Understand that other people are not mind readers. They really don't know something unless you tell them. Remember that people treat you how you treat you. Guess what? Only you know where your shoes hurt. If a colleague relies on your help all the time, that's good because they know they can trust you and count on your help, right? But if you can't offer that help at some point, simply tell her you can't. And do not feel guilty about your refusal to help at that point, or even your refusal to help at all. Use your power of no.

Remember how toddlers say no to everything they don't want or like to do? It's perplexing that even little children know how to use their no's and we as adults don't. I told my 3-year old, "Kemka, can you get my phone please? And he said, "NO." It was a definitive "NO." He didn't want to go to the dinner table and pick up my phone and bring it back to me. So he said "no." And at another time, I said, "Kemka, please give me Kamsi's cup." And he said, "Yes mommy," and brings the cup to me. You see what I mean. Kids are not afraid to say 'no' at least most of the time. So, I suggest you tap into your childhood "no" mindset if it is particularly hard for you as an adult. There is no need to pile lots of things upon our plate just to please everybody. When I began to write this book, I had to literally rethink many of my commitments. I also used my "no" gently but powerfully so I could have time to create this masterpiece.

Sometimes, saying no is easier said than done especially within the family. As family members we think we have the responsibility of carrying each other's burden and pains, which we don't necessarily have to. As an individual, you have to create a boundary or limit that will enable you to excel. Are you are that family member who appears to solve all the problems? Are you there to bail Henry from jail? Are you paying for gas for your sister Sissy or groceries for grandma? Or are you providing accommodation when uncle JP lost his home? Are you paying for auntie Ginger's 50th marriage anniversary celebration? And the list goes on and on. If indeed you are that person then, the truth of the matter is many family members may want to take advantage of your kindheartedness, perhaps not maliciously.

Now, I am not saying that you should not give, but be intentional and conscious when you do give. Don't over burden yourself with other people's luggage even if they are family members. It is ok to say no now or later. It is perfectly fine for you to stop doing all that you have been doing for everybody today, not tomorrow. The moment you realize that you cannot be everything to everybody is the moment you start living and stop existing. From today, assure yourself that you are not going to accept whatever is thrown at you just because they think you can afford it. Live your life by your design. Use your power of no to set much-needed boundaries and set the tone for how people should treat you. Additionally, saying no and using the power does not only apply to physical things and tangible things. It could also mean saying no to that toxic relationship, or saying no to that dead end job. It could mean saying no to your current situation and circumstances, and taking back your life to chart a new course. Remember, knowing makes a whole lot of difference. Thank God, you now know what to do.

Do What You Mean and Mean What You Say

As a parent I can acknowledge that I have given conflicting signals to my children many times. Most times it was unconsciously and sometimes consciously. For instance, I once reprimanded my son for doing something I considered wrong and then he starts crying. And instead of allowing him to cry and get his emotions out, I quickly rushed back to his side to *fix* his cry. I usually start by asking him to stop. Then I beg him to stop. And then I offer him things like juice, milk, apple or anything that will make him stop crying. The child can get really confused and think that doing what he did will always lead to gratification. I have definitely learned my lessons over the years. These days if I reprimand him and he starts crying, it's all fine and good. I let him cry or I send him to the 'crying chair' to fully express his emotion. Whenever he stops, I will sit him down and explain to him why I reprimanded him. And he says, "Am sorry mommy". So, in setting a tone for how other people should treat you, we shouldn't say one thing and do another. It is also important that we exemplify the acceptable behavior that we are trying to promote especially as parents.

Another example, perhaps you go out on a date with someone. From the beginning, you let him know that you do not kiss on first date, and he seems on board with it. Then, after the dinner you begin to cozy up to him, and getting in his space in a manner that is *too close to comfort*. He then reciprocates with a kiss. You start to get angry and begin to withdraw because you told him earlier that you guys are not going to kiss. Of course, you might have said that but your signals said something else. Unfortunately, I don't think you should blame your date for his action because you laid the foundation of confusion preceding the kiss. You can be annoyed and angry with this person all you want, but remember that you gave him conflicting messages and signs. We have to be very clear about what we put out there as well as our expectations.

It is simply wrong to say one thing and do another because most of the time, other people's expectations develop from what they understand from our actions not words. Remember the old saying that, "Actions speak louder than words." Do what you mean and mean what you say. If a family member asks you for money and you cannot afford it or don't want to honor it, please tell that family member "no." Do not give him false hope. And then down the road you start avoiding that person because you do not want to honor your promise. Sometimes, we do these things unknowingly, unconsciously, and unintentionally; however, it is still wrong. It is important that we begin to be fully intentional as regards to communicating our messages and expectations in order to achieve our desired result. Today is the day to begin to allow your actions to speak for you. Let's go and make it happen, today!

Set the Tone on How You Treat Others: The Golden Rule

Having acknowledged that as human beings we are really blessed to have each other and interact with one another. It then becomes necessary, if not imperative, that we treat other people the way we want to be treated, which is with love, kindness and respect. The golden rule says, "Do unto others as you would want them do unto you." Point blank, period! If the whole world can abide by this rule, then I believe half of the world's problems would be solved. This means that most people will be rational, considerate and understanding when dealing with other people, and vice versa. So even in taking back your life, in getting your points across, and in standing up for yourself, you still have to be mindful of how you treat other people. You cannot allow yourself to become arrogant, cocky, demeaning, mischievous or vindictive even if you are setting a tone for your life. This kind of behavior is really not justifiable for any reason whatsoever.

If someone has wronged you in any way, shape or form, pardon and forgive them and find a way to move on. This is one of the lessons that I have struggled with because I felt that maybe the only way to really get my message across was to give that person a taste of his own medicine. I thought that *you treat me bad, then I am going to treat you bad as well, and we keep it moving.* However, after reading and learning from the teachings of Dr. Martin Luther King Jr. this last February during Black History Month, I became completely in awe of how kind and forgiving he was. Dr. King was accepting of all people irrespective of how they treated him. His preaching, messages, and principles reflected this as well. Here is one of his quotes that stuck with me: "You not only refuse to shoot a man, but you refuse to hate him." This powerful quote made me realize the need to forgive beyond rationality. It is a waste of time and energy to have naysayers get a dose of their own medicine. Instead, give them a dose of who you really are, that is your kindness, your love, your compassion and every good that embodies you as person. Keep treating everyone well. One day they will catch up with you or their karma will catch up with them.

There is a famous saying that says, "Every action causes a reaction." However, I say every action should cause an *intentional* reaction because you are responsible for your action and have the right of choice. You choose the way you want to react. The power of choice has not been taken away from you. You still have your God-given power and authority to make decisions, so chose however you want. Period. When you live consciously and intentionally it becomes easier to choose your reaction to actions intentionally, irrespective of foregoing situations and circumstances. The final word here is choice. And thankfully, you have this power but when you allow events and situations to make you act in a certain way, then you are giving your power away. The bottom line is set a tone for how you treat other people by making the golden rule your watchword and see your life elevate. See you at the top my friend.

Chapter 3 Assignments:

Tip: get a pen and your journal or paper if no journal.

1. List and write down all the things you need to forgive yourself for. You know yourself better than anyone, so be truthful as you tackle this task. What do you need forgiveness for? Is it for failing multiple times in business? Not taking actions on your goals? Not doing your best at all times, like being lazy and watching TV all day? Do you need to forgive yourself for when you were molested, abused or raped? Not graduating from college? Not pursuing your dreams? Or maybe some other things I have not mentioned. What is it that you need to forgive yourself for? Feel free to lay it all out on the table.

2. List all the people who you need to forgive. Make a list of people who have wronged you, caused you pain in the past, those who you felt were not there for you, etc.

3. Apart from a spa treatment and shopping, both of these I love by the way, list 10 other ways you are going to intentionally show yourself more love. GO! Remember to include the hashtags #SelfloveList + #POPPEffect, and post it on social media and tag me.☺

4. List the five practical ways you are going to use to forgive the people you listed in number 2 above. For each person, list a way that will work best towards forgiveness. It could be

calling, writing an email, meeting face-to-face, etc. You know the best way to deal with these situations individually. What are you going to do?

5. Finally, write out affirmations regarding the above. For example, *I will focus on the good in every situation. I will choose to speak intentionally in every situation because I have the power.* Begin to affirm the things you want to see happen in your life, and watch how your life takes a turn for the best.

Notes

4

We Only Have 24 hours in a Day

Time Is Ticking

As I write this epic chapter, the clocking is ticking. Time is going, and I am getting older and wiser. Luckily, the same time ticks for everybody. So, no particular person can complain, or be mad, or feel left out as a result of how their time ticks. It is the same 24 hours in a day for everyone; from the presidents to kings to pop stars to moms to dads and even to homeless individuals. This time is on fire or rather it is fire. Time works and works around the clock and ticks and tocks until none of it is left, then it starts over yet again. We all know or rather seem to know about time, that it ticks and go and go, even my three year old is conscious of time. As our home wall clock ticks to signal its constant change, my son points to it, and sometimes he says aloud the new time. How awesome. Even though I have known about the constant change of time and the fact that we get only 24 hours in a day since childhood, it feels like I just realized this last year.

Why didn't I notice that I was wasting my precious time by engaging unintentionally? Why have I always felt like, "Ok, if I don't do it today, I will do it tomorrow" as if tomorrow is promised? And sometimes tomorrow will come and go, so will the next tomorrow, and the day after until the entire week, month and months are wasted. And clearly that job is still undone. But, I thank the almighty God for making me realize the importance of staying faithful to my time. And it is my sincere wish and prayer that you learn from my experiences. If you ever want to get to where you are going, it is highly important that you value your time and be respectful of other people's time as well. As you know, time doesn't wait for you to take action before it ticks. Time is continually ticking whether or not you placed that phone call, or whether that application form is filled out or not. Whether your website is up and running or not, time keeps ticking. Whether or not you have help with childcare so you can concentrate more on your side business, time keeps ticking. The truth is that we all have circumstances that are beyond our control. Does that stop time? NOPE! Time is time. Time is strong. Time is beauty. Time is strength. Time can inspire, invent, innovate, create, and birth. And sometimes time can hinder or stop you. Time is old and time is young.

In other words, any time is a great time to start taking actions towards the goals that we desire to get accomplished. If you feel that you have nothing to accomplish then start something today. You can volunteer, learn how to sing, dance, sew, or how to jump rope. You can start a blog, start writing in your journal, or do whatever you can with the time you have. Time is precious. Again, the most reasonable thing to do would be to outsmart our dear time. Get ahead by planning ahead. Have you asked yourself, *How have the super successful people managed to get more done?*

Discipline

The act of discipline is really important and powerful for managing your time and resources you have to achieve your goal. Being disciplined means that one is able to have self-control or moderation to a certain degree. This simple, but yet powerful, virtue helps us to apply ourselves only to the things that are important at the moment. For instance, you are writing a book that is approximately 10,000 words. And initially, you hoped to finish it in 20 days because you planned to write at least 500 words each day for the next 20 days. However, it is now day 60 and you are still not finished because you have been distracted by circumstances around you. And you find yourself doing everything else except the writing. This is total lack of discipline.

Discipline helps you to fully commit to what you want to do and timely deliver irrespective of life circumstances, trials or temptations. Remember, the things that are important to you can always change from time to time. So, if writing your book is important right now, I suggest you activate your discipline mode and make it happen. This is what the pros do. The people we consider "successful" discipline themselves and are only available to the most important tasks. Begin today to maintain a high level of discipline in most things you have set out to do, and you will marvel at your result. When you lack discipline in your life and in what you do, then it may take more time and more resources to reach your destination. Remember, time is more important than money because we can never refill or buy more time.

Determination

Determination is simply the ability to pursue any given goal firmly and purposefully. This word is not new by any means. It is the same word we have heard and used many times. Unfortunately, sometimes we forget to apply and enforce it in our endeavors. However, professionals and the most successful people always remember to completely apply it. For example, the founder of Kentucky Fried Chicken (KFC), Colonel Sanders, was a determined person who firmly pursued his goal and purpose. I mentioned a little bit about him earlier in the chapter two. When he became certain to build a fried chicken empire, he knocked on door after door, asking restaurants to partner with him. At each restaurant, he would cook his famous original recipe and most of them would eat, shake hands, and say, "Oh we are sorry, not at this this time." But, he kept going and traveled from city to city, and state to state. It is on record that Colonel Sanders received 1009 NOs before his first yes! Talk about a determined man.

How many applications have you submitted and you are already giving up? Or perhaps you are thinking that it cannot be done because it is too much? Please I urge you to press on more firmly and keep sight of that big vision, instead of thinking about the difficulty you are currently going through. Please think about how you will feel when you make it. Rejoice in that joy, happiness and freedom that will come if you accomplish that goal. Remember, it will be here sooner than you know. Decide today to be steadfast with that dream and vision of yours because it is the only way you are going to win.

Dedication

As a parent, we often dedicate ourselves to our kids. We are at their beck and call, especially when they are young. We feed them, bath them, change them, play with them, and buy them new clothing. And we give them many other countless things. Come rain or come shine, we show up for our kids and stay up. We do not show up and disappear. We show up and give them all our attention. I remember how dedicated my mama was with anything and everything that had to do with me. How amazing! How awesome! There has never been a single time that I couldn't count on her. Funny enough, that is how I have dedicated my time, my energy and my resources to serving my kids. I still remember turning down my dream job after I had my son because I wanted to be there and raise him, especially considering the fact that I do not have help. I cannot stress the importance of dedication enough. Remember that what you commit yourself to is what you think about, and what you think about is what you achieve. This reminds us to further devote more time, attention and commitment to our goals.

Again, if we do not have goals, visions or dreams, it wouldn't matter how we spend the 24 hours in our day, right? But because we have lofty goals that we want to achieve in the near future, it becomes paramount that we remain accountable. And the three ways to do this is by ensuring that we are disciplined, determined and dedicated with anything and everything we want to accomplish. Now I know for sure that we have only 24 hours in a day. And when you are disciplined, determined and dedicated towards a course of action, you will then be able to bring it to manifestation. And now I am glad you know this too. Let's go out there and manifest our dreams. Let's make it happen today. We are so worth it! See you at the top my friend.

Chapter 4 Assignments:

Tip: get a pen and your journal or paper if no journal.

1. What is the goal you are pursuing at the moment? Please write it down. If you are not pursuing any particular goal, what is on your mind? (Remember, if you do not have a goal, then it will be impossible to expect anything.)

2. Is it writing a book, an e-book, or an e-course? Making a Freemium? Starting a beauty parlor?

3. Set an accomplishment time and date.

4. What actions are you going to perform daily that will lead to accomplishing this goal?

5. Get an accountability partner. Start!

Notes

_____

_____

_____

_____

_____

_____

_____

_____

_____

_____

_____

_____

_____

_____

_____

_____

_____

_____

_____

5

The Mind Is Very Powerful

My Mind Is Powerfully Positive

I now realize that the mind is powerful, more powerful than I would have ever understood or imagined. In fact, the mind is a super power, an originator of dreams and visions, the conceiver of ideas, and the executor of goals. The mind is indeed a creator, a producer, an innovator, a fabricator, and an inventor. The mind forms, shapes and constructs thoughts and intentions into a feasible possibility. Before any vision or dream can come true physically, you would have manifested it in your mind. If you truly cannot conceptualize your vision, dreams or goals in the spirit realm or in your mind, then you may never be able to truly manifest those things physically.

This is because we first build in our minds, everything we want and desire. We must first bring our desires into existence by the power of our mind. This is why we have to concentrate on the things we want to see happen in our lives. We have to cultivate and pour into what we want to reap. We want to make sure to dream our dreams into existence by mindfully focusing on them. The funny thing is that I have heard many experts say this repeatedly about the mind being all of that. And to be honest I didn't quite understand it until recently. The truth of the matter is that you may have heard it as well. But, I am here to reinforce it for you because maybe, just like me, you heard this truth a couple of months or years ago, and you need that re-awakening as you read this today. Almost everything in life starts first with our mind. Some people call this our head or heart or even intuition or gut feeling. Irrespective of what you call it, everything begins with thoughts and ideas from your mind.

In life, how you start doesn't necessarily equal how you end.

Let's take a look at the life of Albert Einstein. As a teenager, Einstein failed to reach the standard requirements for entrance into the Swiss Federal Polytechnic in Zurich at 16-years old, even though excelling in mathematics and physics on the exam. He would end up attending a different school because of his failure to reach the basic acceptable standard of entrance. From there,

Einstein went to a four-year college to study mathematics and physics, which were his passion and desires at that time. At only 17, he knew he had to focus on his passions, interests, strengths, and his areas of predominance. He had to concentrate on the areas that fascinate him, which was mathematics and physics. Both subjects aroused his enthusiasm and attention. He took it, embraced it and acted upon it. When people praised him for having special talent, he explained, "I have no special talent. I am only passionately curious." He never wasted a day trying to figure out things that did not interest him. This guy is a genius. I remember wasting three good weeks trying to figure out how to set up a simple WordPress blog! What??? Eventually, I hired someone from Upwork for only $50.00, and he had it up and running within 72 hours. This experience taught me so much.

Too many times we seem to write ourselves off when we fail in one area. It is important that we understand that failing in one area doesn't mean failing in all areas. It is important that we channel our mind towards the things that will build us up, the places where our strengths lie. This is true unless we really want to learn, refine, improve, and enhance our weakness. That is, we are so interested in that area that we are willing to do anything to right the wrongs. If that's the case then bravo, let the learning begin. However, if that's not the case, then please focus on your interest, embrace it and give it opportunity to shine. The last thing you want to be is a jack of all trades. Again, this does not mean that when we begin to focus on our strengths it will be all rosy and smooth sailing. No, there are still trials, temptations and tribulations. Things can still go wrong and we may still fail. This is why the most important thing is our ability to get right back up after each fall.

Mentally, in the young Albert Einstein's mind, he believed he can and he was willing to do more to get the result he wanted. He explains in one of his speeches that, "It's not that I'm so smart, it's just that I stay with problems longer." Keywords: **stay with problems longer!** We have to be willing to do more in order to find the solutions that we need. We have to do more in order to solve those problems that will get our lives, dreams, and visions to the next level. We simply cannot do the same thing and expect a different result. That's the definition of insanity. If you want more you have to do more, period. Start realizing that your mind is powerful. Begin to be mindful of what you feed it because your mind will grow on what you feed it. If you want more in life, then you have to feed your mind the right food that will enable it to create, elevate and grow. This truth I now know for sure.

Your Perception Will Define You

Have you ever wondered if your line of thinking or perception can actually change your cause of action? I will say heck YAY!! You may already know; perception is a mental impression, which leads to attention, concentration and action. But then, the power of positive perception helps you to look at life positively, what this means is that you view your circumstances and situations affirmatively. And unfortunately, if you choose to view them negatively then that's what you will see in your surroundings. Positive perception can be a life changer for you. It can totally change the cause of actions in your life because what you dwell upon, and how you dwell upon it, is what you become. Have you heard the phrase 'think big if you are going to be thinking at all' a famous quote by Donald Trump? My question to you is how do you perceive your environment? Or better still, how do you think about your environment? The word "environment" here means your life, your job, your situation, your circumstances, etc., Are you seeing your situation as the worst and there is nothing you can do about it? And are you ok with being at the bottom? Or are you hopeful that things will change and are working to ensure that things change?

I want to encourage you to begin to see yourself in the direction you want to go, even if you may not be there yet. Be determined to work with what you have at the moment to get yourself to where you want to be. The truth is you have to put in the work; don't let people tell you otherwise. And another truth is that you can absolutely change your situation, and it starts with changing your perception. One of the most fascinating stories of all time is the story of Napoleon Hill and how the change in his thoughts permanently changed the course of his life. Many times we conceive, create and develop powerful dreams in our minds and it ends up not seeing the light of the day because of negative limiting beliefs. But the good news is that we can change. Yes, you can change and I can change. Change starts from what you think about and how you think about it. Today, change how you see things and you will see how change will begin to happen in your corner of the world. The key takeaway from this chapter is that seeing things in a positive light can make a positive change, which could be all you need to elevate your life and make a positive impact. See you at the top my friend.

Chapter 5 Assignments:

Tip: get a pen and your journal or paper if no journal.

1. How are you going to physically make the changes in your thinking or perception as discussed in the chapter? (I want you to be really mindful and intentional here. Are you going to get off your couch and start doing instead of trying? Maybe it's that website or Amazon store? Start writing that book, that blog post, etc.

2. What steps are you going to take every day to constantly think in a positive way considering that we witness trials, temptation and tribulations daily? Please don't over think these "steps." It could simply be developing virtues like patience, compassion, love, beauty, joy, happiness, etc.

3. Finally, write out two or three affirmative words if you believe in affirmations. For example, *I am in control of my mind, my thoughts and my actions. I will focus on healthy thinking irrespective of what is thrown at me. I will see love, peace and beauty in my life and circumstances regardless of the situation,* etc.

Notes

6

Everybody Has an Opinion

Opinion Is the Lowest Form of Human Intelligence

Remember Bill Bullard's saying, "opinion is the lowest form of human knowledge or intelligence," and that everyone has one. I have heard the above saying thousands of times before now, and I didn't quite understand what it really meant. In the past, I have seen myself question why people should have an opinion regarding my situation. The fact is that everybody has an opinion including kids who express their "yeses" and "no's" as many times as possible during the day. So truly knowing, or rather understanding, that everyone has opinion has helped me in the recent months. And I hope it sets you free as well. So instead of asking, "Why you gotta have an opinion about my stuff?" You can now say, "That's ok if that's how you see it but I am sticking with my plans." I love "but's."

So, before now I have seen myself change my plans because of people's opinions. I have seen myself give up on the things I consider to be important because of peoples advise. I have seen myself settle because of people's recommendations. But now, I have come to know better; and one of the things that I now know for sure is that everyone has an opinion. And I have decided that opinions will not stop me again because they do not matter much anyway. Are you allowing other peoples' thoughts and opinions about you to bother you like I used to? Are you allowing their expressed fears and concerns stop you? Remember, you are the only one that knows your dreams, goals and intentions. Be aware that people may not necessarily fully understand what you are going though or how you want to show up in life until everything starts to manifest. Maybe you shouldn't be wasting your precious time considering their opinions of your situation if in fact they do not really understand. Also, beware of naysayers that have nothing good to say even when they seem to understand. The only opinion that really matters is your opinion; your opinion about your situation and circumstances; your opinion about your visions, dreams and goals.

Know Who You Are

Take inventory of yourself, situations and circumstances, and then tell yourself the truth and accept it. When you know the truth about your situations and circumstances, then, what people think of them wouldn't bother you. Remember you have the facts. They are working with hearsay and you are working with Certified Truthful Facts; I call it CTF for short. Let's look at opinions this way. As long as a human being has a functional brain, then she will definitely see something in a certain way, good or bad. Do you agree with me? Therefore, it is perfectly ok for that person to have an opinion. You are not in control of opinions anyway. So, what else are you going to do about that? NOTHING! Basically, the only thing to do is not allow it to bother you. Understand that other people's opinions are rightly their opinion. And you do not have control over it except to not let it stop you in any way, shape or form.

Power of Purposeful Perseverance

The great Amelia Earhart was diagnosed with *chronic sinusitis* after she became sick while working as a nurse aide with the Volunteer Aid Detachment that helped the troops during World War I. The doctors were of the opinion that her *chronic sinusitis* would affect her flying activities but Amelia never allowed that situation to stop her. The fact is that some opinions may be valid, logical or a true concern. However, you still have the final say regarding your situation. No one can take your power of decision-making away from you unless you let them. You are the architect of your dreams and goals. If you pay no mind to that opinion, it will die a natural death. I have started to do this with my own life because I know I have my best interests at heart.

Do you know the motive behind certain opinions? Then why should you be bothered by it? Why lose sleep over someone or something that is not entirely true or something that doesn't necessarily define you? Even when such opinions are genuine, remember that you are still the boss of your life, and you should not allow anyone else to make decisions about your life. Let's go back to the story of the great Amelia Earhart. The doctors had genuine concern about her chronic condition. So what? Nevertheless, she remained focused on her vision, dreams and goals. She focused on the things she knew for sure. She focused on the journey, the things she could change and the result she wanted to see. She never thought to stop what she wanted to accomplish because of that situation. And she went ahead to achieve many aviation records including the first person to fly solo from Honolulu, Hawaii to Oakland, California; the first woman to fly solo nonstop across the Atlantic; and many more in her short life.

The current president of Liberia, Ms. Eileen Sirleaf Johnson, is another example of someone who modeled the power of purposeful perseverance behavior. She closed her ears against all opinions, logical and illogical, because she understood her dream & vision. Unfortunately, some people may never understand the magnitude of the dream that has been given to them or even its urgency. But, my prayer is that this will not be you! Sometimes, people will urge you to wait, but you know in your heart it is the time to start! This is the time to act! Since the best time to ever begin any project is NOW! Ms. Sirleaf Johnson felt a strong calling to serve her people. Yet each time she tried, she would hit a road block, and get knocked to the ground. But, she got right back up, dusted off the stains and started yet again.

Remember, she wasn't born into a rich and famous family. Even as a child, she had a desire to serve, help people and do her best. The road to this dream was never a smooth sailing. Married at 17-years-old, sentenced to years in a Liberian prison multiple times, and yet she kept her purpose alive. She powered through while persevering against all odds. In 1961, she traveled to the United States to study, and she earned an associate degree in accounting from Madison Business School. She then received a

Masters of Public Administration from Harvard University. She went back to her home country of Liberia after receiving her Master's degree, and eventually became an Assistant Minister of Finance. However, she never stopped or took her eyes off her vision of one day becoming the president of her country. Time after time she tried again and again, never giving up, even when she was faced with multiple prison sentences, jail time and incarcerations. She was not deterred because she knew and understood the power behind her purpose.

On January 16, 2006, she became the first female president of Liberia and the first female president ever elected in Africa. So, I truly think there are many lessons to learn here. One of them is we can only be stopped by the opinions of others if we cultivate, water, groom and harvest those opinions. Another lesson is the importance of clarity of purpose. Knowing your vision and goal is important and being very clear about them is even more important. Sometimes, this knowledge makes the difference between going all in for something you firmly believe in or allowing the opinions of others to stop you. My question to you is what are you going to do? Of course, I will definitely encourage you to go out there and do whatever it takes to accomplish your dream because your dreams can come true only if you act upon them. As often said, *clarity comes by engagement*, so you have engage or act. There's no other way. Believe you can and begin to act. In other words, Get up! Take an action to make an impact. See you at the top my friend.

Chapter 6 Assignments:

Tip: get a pen and your journal or paper if no journal

1. Mirror work: Look at yourself in the mirror without makeup and with all your flaws. See through who you are and accept yourself the way you are. (I learned this trick from my friend Yi-An Lee of **http://www.yianlee.com**)

2. Write down your strengths: the things that come to you easily or the things you are good at.

3. Write down your weaknesses: the things you need help mastering.

4. Be willing to accept yourself for who you are at this moment and be willing to work on yourself to become the best you possible. Decide to not allow an opinion to hinder you today.

5. Take an action that exemplifies your power of purposeful perseverance irrespective of people's opinions. It could be finally starting a new job or career, relocating or just going to a movie.

Notes

7

Rain Falls on Every Roof

Rain Comes and Goes

An African proverb says "rain does not fall on one roof alone," even though this proverb is not literally talking about rain. Yet, if you decide to apply it literally, it means that when it rains there is the likelihood that your neighbor's house will be touched by it. In other words, it's highly impossible that rain falls only on your roof. I have never seen this happen ever. And I don't think anyone has. Sometimes the houses down the road will be touched slightly, heavily or may even be spared by that rain. Perhaps, the surrounding cities will get their own rain at the same time as your city or at different time. But, the truth of the matter is that every roof will experience rain at some point in time. And when it happens, it won't be happening just on that roof alone.

Each year thousands of people graduate from colleges. Thousands of people also become medical doctors, teachers, social workers, police officers, bankers, inventors, innovators, speakers and writers. And, of course, thousands of people have problems and go through lots of bad things as well. I want you to remember that no matter what you may be going through right now, you are not alone. There are many people like you out there who are going through the same stuff in this big, beautiful world. Don't ever think that you are alone. Don't ever think that the world has forsaken you. Don't ever think that your troubles are the worst. There is always someone somewhere having it worse down the road. But one thing I want you to understand is that the world is changing. It will be cool if you start adjusting your view and begin to make a conscious shift as the world changes. Start to remodel the information you have to fit into where you want to go. There is enough for everybody. Just like life happens to everyone, opportunities abound for everyone as well.

The world is a big place that can comfortably fit all our gigantic ideas and innovations. Yet, in today's world, technology has made it seem smaller, now that everything happens in an instant. There are instant messages, instant calls, and people see your tweets as soon as you click *send*. With emails, voice mails, and apps, it feels like there are endless things that keeps us busy in an already busy world. It feels like we no longer have an excuse not to be successful or reach our full potential because the world offers so much opportunity at this time. Yet, it also feels like all these distractions and busy lifestyles are excuses that can derail our destiny. As I continue on this path of personal development and realization, I have come to understand many things for sure.

One of the things I now know for sure is that everybody goes through something at one point or another. It may be not at the same time. Things happen. Most of the time it is not about the things that happen to you, but rather how you manage and react to the things that happen. This is because we have the ability to push beyond the rain, beyond the troubles, beyond the trials, and beyond every temptation in our lives. Remember, rain comes and goes. If you see everything from this perspective then, you will be victorious. Irrespective of what you may be witnessing at this point, regardless of the heaviness of the rain falling all over your roof right now, I urge you to remember that life happens to everyone and you are not alone. Most importantly, this too shall pass.

Before now, I used to be so afraid of everything. And sometimes I just feel like "OMG, my situation is the worst," "I can't take a break," "someone is after me or my life." But now I do know, and I know for sure, that it rains on every roof and there is no need to trouble my peace. And there is no need to take it personal either. Now, I know for sure that no condition is ever permanent; bad things shall pass away, good things shall pass away. At the end, what is most important is your ability to persevere through it all.

Remaining Unstoppable #NoExcuse

Every excuse is a legit excuse at least from the point of view of the excuser, but still no excuse is excusable. Mother Teresa of Calcutta was born poor in Macedonia and at a very young age she desired to be a nun. It was said that part of her inspiration came from listening to stories about missionaries and religious people who lived a life of service to others. One of the earliest and hardest hindrances she pushed through was leaving home at the young age of 18; this was huge then and still huge today. This kind of decision is not an easy feat. Leaving home at 18 to pursue your purpose was difficult but the young Mother Teresa had a very strong conviction about her purpose and journey, therefore nothing could stop her.

Not only was she leaving home to go and pursue this "uncertain" future, she was also moving to another country that doesn't speak her language. And, she is going to learn how to speak English because it was the language of the sisters of Loreto.

The problem that confronted young Mother Teresa at 18-years-old was serious, and for some of us it could have become an end to our dream and vision. But, she kept sight of her finish line and continued with patience and great determination. She knew that nothing ever stays the same and eventually this too shall pass away. Of course, it did pass and she became a nun in 1937. She was assigned to teach children in Calcutta, India. And it was there that she witnessed the poorest of the poor and made another life-changing decision. She wanted to go and serve this group of people - the downtrodden, the forsaken of society, the sickly and the people that were deserted by family. She strongly believed that she was called to minister to them. In 1948, she officially began her ministry with the poor. It was then that she witnessed one of her hardest struggles ever, the struggle within her spirit and the temptation to go back to the comfort of the Loreto convent.

Situations were really tough during the start of her ministry. She mainly begged for supplies, food and other things she needed to support the poor. One day as she walked several miles within her new community to look for a home, it dawned on her how much this poor people travel looking for food, home, and healthcare access and how much the body can take. She was tempted to abandon this new ministry of the poor and walk right back into the convent. But she fought that temptation with every bit of strength and the Holy Spirit. At the end, she stayed true to her purpose and destiny.

Defeat the Competition

As human beings, sometimes we are unconsciously forced to look over our shoulders to check and see how our neighbor is doing. We look to determine whether or not she is doing better than us, and maybe figure out what she is using and the people who are helping her. Sometimes, this kind of behavior can be exhibited innocently and other times maliciously or competitively. Irrespective of your intent, if you are that sister or brother who demonstrates this kind of behavior whether naively or perspicuously, I will advise you to check yourself. Work to become more conscious and pump the breaks to stop whenever you catch yourself stepping into this kind of behavior. My personal thought about competition with other people is that it is bad - point blank, period. I totally do not like competition and cannot stand it. The only competition I can second is when you compete with yourself. For instance, when you increase your exercise and physical activity tempo to enable you do better today than you did yesterday.

When you compete with yourself, it helps you to get better. On the contrary, when you begin to compete and compare yourself, your life and your businesses with other people around you, then it may lead to resentment and unhealthy rivalries. Put differently, competition can easily kill the fun in anything. I remember growing up in Africa, sometimes our parents will say, "Don't you see Jessie, your Elementary school classmate, now she is a pharmacist, married with 3 children and you don't have none. What are you waiting for?" Our parents, aunties and uncles are probably coming from a place of love. However, unfortunately, this kind of talk can stir up unnecessary competition, which is unhealthy by the way. Sometimes as parents, we may push our kids to the extent they may begin to resent us. Before, I thought that competition could help me get better. But actually, the reverse is the case because competition can do more harm than good to you.

And as long as you are planning to walk in your purpose and destiny, you really need to stay away from looking at your neighbor's, friend's, sister's, acquaintance's or even strangers' lives. It is paramount for you to remember that everyone is running a separate race in this lifetime. Therefore, there is no need to compete all you need do is to focus on your lane. You can end up in a different destination than originally intended if you keep looking over your shoulder. And then, you are going to need extra gas, time and money to fix it.

Even if you did not get anything from this chapter, I really want you to now know for sure that life happens to everybody. So, therefore, do not take whatever you are going through right now to be personal because it will surely pass away too. I urge you to always remain patient and focused on your journey, as it is different from anyone else's. See you at the top my friend.

Chapter 7 Assignments:

Tip: get a pen and your journal or paper if no journal

Please take 15-30 minutes break to relax. During this break:

1. Remind yourself that life happens to everybody and you are not alone.

2. Write down three ways you can collaborate with someone in your niche or even another niche. For example, this could be as a blog guest, interview an expert, a referral, etc.

3. List the actual businesses that you want to collaborate with regarding the services listed in number 2 above.

4. Contact these businesses by emails, phone, etc.

5. Good luck!

Notes

_____

_____

_____

_____

_____

_____

_____

_____

_____

_____

_____

_____

_____

_____

_____

_____

_____

_____

_____

8

Be a Believer to See

Seeing Is Believing?

Ok, I have heard the quote, "seeing is believing," over and over again. And I know you have as well, so please do not tell me you have not. The truth of the matter is that I have heard it more than 500 times to say the least. And one issue I have noticed is that as you begin to hear everyone echo, "seeing is believing," you begin to believe it too. Unfortunately, that is the reality in the world today; majority of the people wants to see evidence before they believe. Thank goodness I am here to help you perceive and understand another reality. What if you believe before you see, just like the Bible instructed in John 20:29? What do you think will happen? Do you really think your faith can activate what you have not seen? Of course YES! One of the things that I have come to now know to be true and for sure is that "seeing is not always believing." I also know that we can confidently believe the goodness and love and mercy and beauty and success that we want to see come to fulfillment in our life before they become our reality. As a matter of fact, it is even more important that we believe before we see. My tip is to believe and act with conviction.

What the Mind Can Conceive and Believe, It Can Achieve

"Whatever the mind can conceive and believe, it can achieve" this statement was made famous by Napoleon Hill. He explained how as human beings we have the ultimate power to change our thought processes and then change our lives for the better. Even though this was years ago, this law will still very much apply to your life and situation today!

10 Million Dollars in the Making

Jim Carrey is an American actor and comedian. He started at a very early age, performing in school for his classmates and teacher. He had a tough childhood growing up. At one point, his father lost his job, and Jim and his family had to live in a camper van on their uncle's lawn. As a result, everyone in the family had to get a job, so he officially started working at 15-years-old. He would eventually drop out of high school the next year to pursue this career. He went to Hollywood at 19, and there he realized that making it is like the biblical saying in Matthew 19:24 of the *camel passing through the eye of a needle*. It was never going to be as easy. He got to a very low point in his life. And as he reflected on his situation, he decided to take a life-changing action. He reached for his checkbook, and wrote himself a future check for 10 million dollars for "acting services rendered." He believed before he saw. At the time he wrote the check, he knew he couldn't afford his basic needs, but he believed that in the future he definitely would make 10 million dollars. He never judged himself based on his present situation nor thought that his life would never recover. He blatantly refused to believe his present circumstances were to be his final situation. He knew he would make it and that his life and circumstances would change. And it did.

Over the next 10 years he made that money from a series of movies, *Ace Ventura: Pet Detective* and *Dumb and Dumber*. For this guy, believing and acting towards that goal led him to his results. It is important to see from the eyes of faith. Faith without work is dead, so you have to put in the work. Everyone that seeks growth and elevation has to put in the work. For instance, irrespective of how great my faith is in believing that I will be a best-selling author. However, I never actually sit down to write a book, then that dream may never be realized. So, today I ask you to activate your faith by fully and truly believing in the dream you have conceived. Begin to act towards that purpose, by starting with actions that need to be done. If this means taking some things off your plate, then do it. If it means working late hours, then do it. If it means less time on Facebook and other social media, then do it. Do not allow this hour to pass without you taking a drastic action towards your destiny and purpose like Jim Carrey did. Aspire. Imagine. Work. Reiterate. See you at the top my friend.

Chapter 8 Assignments:

Tip: get a pen and your journal or paper if no journal

1. How much are you going to write on your check for your future self today?

2. What prophesy are you going to release into your life today? For example, in the next six months, "I want to be a published author". Or maybe you want to open your own online social media business, etc. My prophesy was in January 2016 when I told myself that before my July 2016 birthday, I will be a published author, and it happened. So, please release your prophesy.

3. What are the ways you are going to make numbers 1 and 2 above happen? List at least two endeavors; it could be acting, singing, blogging, starting your own business (salon, online business, coaching, marketing, etc.).

Notes

_____

_____

_____

_____

_____

_____

_____

_____

_____

_____

_____

_____

_____

_____

_____

_____

_____

_____

_____

_____

_____

9

Start! Inspiration Will Come.

Start Where You Are

One of the things I now know for sure is that I do not have to wait for inspiration to come before I start, which is what I used to do. The truth is that when you start, inspiration will come. As human beings, sometimes we are tempted to have everything figured out before we start, which is not always the right cause of action. Ok, I am not saying that you should not plan, but do not allow your planning and preparation to stop you from proceeding or taking the next step of action. I have seen projects halted because of unnecessary waiting for everything to be "right" or fall in place. Forgive me if you are a writer but I have seen writers do this the most. I have seen writers wait and wait and wait. Nothing is written. Nothing is published because there were no *inspirations*. I have heard some writers share that they always want to go into hiding when they want to begin to write. Some say they have gone or vanished into the woods or rural areas to get inspiration for their books. And I really think it is a great idea because it enables you to fully commit to the project and get it done.

But, what if you don't have the luxury to be away from your family, kids and responsibilities? What if you do not have another place you can go to get the inspiration that you are looking for; for instance, a tree house, a relatives' home who lives in the rural area or even something as simple as a basement? What if all you have is your one bedroom you share with your spouse/partner and kids? What if all you have is a shared room in family house you share with other relations? What if the physical conditions are not conducive and you still have this burning desire to write? You must start where you are, NOW! Find a way to make what you have work for you. Go to library, and write there. Write in the middle of the night when everyone else is sleeping. This moment is what you have; do not waste it waiting for what you do not have. Make this moment count for you.

And I have been guilty of this myself, so I speak from a familiar place. There was a time in my life that I waited for inspirations to write my blog posts. So funny, right? Waiting for inspiration for blog post but this is a true story. And I witnessed a situation in which I never posted on my blog for months because

I was waiting for this powerful golden inspiration that would change the entire universe. I forgot the most important thing. I forgot that I needed to start where I was. I forgot that inspiration is everywhere including where I was at that time. All I need to do is change my perception so I can see the blessings around me and be inspired by them. So, if you are still like me in the past, waiting for that golden nugget, believe that you already have it, and begin to use what you have. Start where you are, and use what you have to get where you want to go. Inspiration is in this moment. Why wait for the next moment that you are not sure of and don't have yet? Why wait for tomorrow that is not promised? Why waste the moment you have waiting for the moment you don't have and the moment you can't guarantee? Please don't do it. It is a bad idea.

Create Your Own Inspiration

One thing I now know for sure is that you can create your own inspiration. Oh YES! You can! I really do think that inspiration is everywhere, but sometimes our busy, noisy world can create unnecessary distractions. We live in a world that is unconsciously loud, music is played out very loud, social media accounts are perpetually open on the phones, and notification alerts are on all day long. Distractions hammer in from front, back, left, right and center. And if you are not careful, you can get trapped by this oversight.

For so long, I wanted to write but my kids and the housework like cooking, cleaning, laundry, etc. would always take over. And by the time I realized it, the day is gone and another day and then another day. When I joined social media, I quickly realized that managing multiple social media accounts equally became another job by itself. This became a sad circle. And I eventually got tired of going through the same sad circle every day and decided to create my own inspiration and outcome. And on April 1, 2016, I became determined to write this book and I started. I gave myself an ultimate deadline, and became resolved to meet it. I started from the things I can control. I shut down noises from social media by turning off my notification alerts, and assigning times to get on the platforms that I use. This action opened up a couple of creative hours during the day. I began to work in the middle of the night as well. I would go to bed 11 p.m. and wake up at 4 a.m., which gives me five hours of sleep and three good hours to work before the kids got up at 7 a.m. You and I can moderate the noises around us to make room for the important things that need our attention.

If you ever find yourself in a similar situation as described above, please think of a way to create your own inspiration.

Remember, you are the only one who knows your dream and you are the driver of your destiny. Therefore, it is your sole responsibility to make sure your dream comes to fruition. The very common phrase you see in most children's program is "Do It Yourself." So, I want urge you to create your own inspiration if you really need to be inspired to attain your creative space and freedom. Ensure that you find a way to motivate yourself so that you can begin and finish without looking back. Quit blaming it on your situation. Your situation is not beyond your capability. You are created and powerfully equipped to handle the stumbling block that you see. Begin to see beyond your problems and be ready to push until there are no more walls blocking you from your destiny.

Inspire the World by Starting

You will agree with me that the world needs more love, kindness, blessings, and many more positive vibes because there are so much negativity going on already. We need more positivity, and as long as what you are trying to start is something good, then there is definitely room for it in the world today. Don't waste all your precious time conceptualizing how your plan is going to unfold. In my opinion, the most important thing is for you to start. As you begin, the plan will start to unfold right in front of you. For instance, I really do not think that the creator of Facebook, Mark Zuckerberg, ever understood how much change his application would bring to world before he started. But, look at Facebook today. It is worth billions of dollars and many people have been inspired by it, and many other apps have been built as a result of it. It is unimaginable how much inspiration you can give to others around you when you finally summon the courage to begin. Today, make a decision to start. Make a decision to inspire your own world and the world of others that will be marveled by your creation.

Your take away from this chapter is that you don't need inspiration to start. Start and inspiration will come, and that is what I have come to now know for sure. I also know that inspiration is everywhere, look around you. In this moment right now, there are many things that can inspire and brighten you. Finally, remember you are the main character in your play of life and you can definitely create your own inspiration. Oh yes, you can. Everything is possible, only if you believe. See you at the top my friend.

Chapter 9 Assignments:

Tip: get a pen and your journal or paper if no journal.

1. Write down five ways you are going to create inspiration. It could be taking a walk, praying, meditating, and tech off (shutting off all electrical appliances, etc.).

2. Write down ways to create more time to enable you to continue in your purpose. What are you going to take off your plate today?

3. Do you really need all the different social media accounts? And are you using them for business? If yes, how can you better manage them to save you some time to work on your purpose? Consider using *Hootsuite* or *Buffer*, both are social media managing platforms that can help you with planning and scheduling your posts ahead of time.

Notes

10

You Have Everything You Need to Begin Now

Time Is Ripe

Many a time a person can go through all the process of changing her life by meticulously doing all the work to get herself in the right frame of mind. She could listen to the right personal development tapes or CDs or read the best self-help books. Yet, when it comes to taking the required action, she may still decide to wait a little bit. I am sure you are familiar with what I am trying to describe here. I have been in a situation whereby I took actions later rather than sooner because I said to myself, "You know the time is not yet ripe." Does time ripe like bananas, avocados and other delicious fruits and vegetables? Well, I digress. I know you know where I am going with that one.

However, I am here today to tell you that you have everything you need to begin at this moment including a ripe time. This is what I now know for sure, time is ripe when it is time. And my dear, good friend reading this amazing book, now is the time because NOW is what you have. Therefore, you actually owe it to yourself, to God and to the universe to start and not while away this precious moment by waiting for a magic occasion. They say *clarity comes by engagement*. Here, *engagement* means *starting* and you can start by watering the ground. For instance, begin to research the business you are planning to start, interview people that have done well in the area that you want go into. You could begin to interview pro-bloggers if you want to be a blogger. Or you could interview and/or talk to a writer if you are planning on becoming one. Engagement can also mean taking the first step to do a Periscope broadcast even when you are not certain about the topics you would want to talk about. You can begin by getting to know your audience, building your community. And if you started out "scoping" (short for Periscoping) about business development, you could end up talking mainly about inspiration if that is what your audience wants. If you never start, you will never know.

What if you never actually started on Periscope? Instead, in preparation to start, you went ahead and built a course, an expensive business development course because in your mind that is what you want to talk about. And by the time you begin, it turned out that your audience wanted inspiration and motivations instead. As a result, your business development course did not sell very well. What are you going to do? So, I want to encourage you to step out on faith and take the first step, even when you are not clear about every single detail of that dream or vision. Do it anyway. As you prepare to begin to live the life you desire, remember that you have everything you need at this time start. You do. Your intelligence is exceptional, your mind is right and focused, your head is ready and you are feeling this intense burning desire to make a change in the world today. I urge you to go for it and never look back.

Trust In Today

Today is the first of its kind. It's a day of harmony, happiness and hope! A day that will be like no other on the face of the earth. It's a day of awakening because you now know that action trumps over every idea. Today is an action day. Are you wondering how to make today count for you? Are you still thinking what makes it different from yesterday? Well, the only way to make it work for you and make it different from yesterday is to do something different today. Do something different towards your dreams. Remember it will always be a dream until you start living it!

The author of the Harry Potter books, who became an "overnight" millionaire, and sold millions of copies and rose to instant fame, lived in her dreams for many years. Until one day she decided to put her foot down and finish her first Harry Potter novel. I bet the day she made that decision was and could still be the best day of her life.

Your "Willpower" Is Like No Other

The human will, just like the human spirit, is powerful and like no other. Why, you may ask? Because we are created in the likeness of the Almighty God. When I talk about *will* here I am referring to your why. It is the reason or the why behind your story, your business, your present situation, your goals, your purpose, your vision and mission. Why are you doing what you are doing? And why do you want to embark on more? It is important to know your *why* because it is the *will*, and it will drive you to accomplishment. Again, when I talk about *willpower* I am referring to a purpose pusher, that volition, strength, resolution and determination that will propel you to execute, achieve and conquer. I am referring to that will of power that you have inside of you, which every one of us has. And if activated, it is able to crystalize you into your greatness.

How do I know if I have willpower? How do I know if it actually exists? All you need to do is recognize that your *willpower* actually does exist. From today onward, I want you to know for sure that this willpower does exist in you. When you know better you do better, so now you know! The next step towards activating your willpower is to believe in God, in yourself and in your abilities. Believe that God made you enough and that you can do it. Sometimes, we give up so easily especially when we take up a new venture, new businesses or when we step out of our comfort zone. Because we don't necessarily believe that we can do it, or we think we are not able to, we end up quitting and starting over and over again. Even though you do have the power to start over whenever you want, doing so very frequently can cause distractions, stress and anxiety.

Today, I urge you to start and stay motivated to accomplish what you have started. Tell yourself that you will follow through because what you have inside you can sustain you to the end. The final step towards activating your willpower is to trust your willpower. Today, I ask you to trust God and yourself. Trust that what God has deposited in you is enough to lead you throughout your journey. Trust with all your heart and do not waiver no matter how tough the going becomes. A high level of trust can only strengthen your will and drive you to keep going.

"All our dreams can come true, if we have the courage to pursue them." This quote was made famous by Walt Disney who started from a humble beginning. The truth of the matter is *where there is a will there is a way*. You probably have heard this quote as well. In most cases, our will drives our strength to go beyond physical pain, distress, trouble, discomfort and any other stumbling blocks out there. Your will is equally able to drive you out of your comfort zone in order for you to step into your greatness. It is easy to think that staying in a comfortable terrain is what you have been called to do. However, the truth is that in order to grow, you have to start being comfortable with being uncomfortable. Remember, your willpower is absolutely able to aid you in whatever you want to do from start to completion. This is what I now know for sure.

People Are Purpose Pushers

One of the things I now know for sure is that the Almighty created abundance within and among us. In His infinite wisdom and understanding, He positioned people to work for your purpose. And today I feel the urgent and serious need to start this paragraph by reminding you about this truth because sometimes we forget. You do have people around you who will always work in your favor to lift you up, inspire and encourage you. This type of people will listen and find the time to grace and bless you with their presence when it gets tough. God has planted people in your live for the sole purpose of your elevation. Be sure to look very closely around you and take advantage of these blessings.

Also, I want to acknowledge that sometimes starting off could seem really unreal, difficult and hard to anyone and everyone. Therefore, do not take it personal. Remember that constant practice makes perfect, and you learn more when you struggle than when everything goes very smooth for you. Open your eyes, and listen up and listen hard for the beautiful lessons in your struggles. And one thing that actually makes it easier for us is that we have other people to look at. There is always going to be someone that has gone that path before. There is always going to be another person that knows a thing or two more than you. You can enter your question into Google or YouTube, if you like video demonstrations, and most of this information is available for free. You can always take a step further to invest in others to get some exclusive info. But you seriously have everything you need to begin.

For instance, if you want to be an international motivational speaker like Tony Robbins or Les Brown, and you want to be trained by them through one of their mentoring or certification programs, it will cost you. There is always a price to pay in exchange for what we truly desire. Nothing good comes for free on this earth except the things that have been given to us by the almighty God. Again, remember that you have everything you need at this moment to begin. Do not waste any more time because there is no more time to be wasted. Trust God. Trust yourself. Trust today and begin. See you at the top my friend.

Chapter 10 Assignments:

Tip: get a pen and your journal or paper if no journal

1. Think of a short-term project you can start today. Short-term could be as little as four weeks or as long as nine months but not a year.

2. What is it? For me, it was this book, I gave myself 90 days. So, think of something that you will see the result in at least 90 days.

3. Get an accountability partner who is preferably a neutral person who will always check on you to ensure your progress.

4. Stay committed with this project by being willing to motivate yourself and check in with your accountability partner weekly.

5. Be sure to breakdown your project in simple tasks.

6. Write out your daily tasks for easy check-in and accountability. For instance, if you are writing a book of 10,000 words, how many words do you need to write every day in order to finish it within four weeks? Approximately 335 words per day should be your daily goal towards this project until it is completed.

7. Ensure to map out time to work on your project daily. For instance 1hr everyday.

8. Finally, congratulations on reading this book! Yes, you did it! Now is the implementation time. Let's go **CREATE GROW & ELEVATE!**

See you at the top my friend.

END

Notes

_____

_____

_____

_____

_____

_____

_____

_____

_____

_____

_____

_____

_____

_____

_____

_____

_____

_____

_____

_____

Acknowledgements

The Journey of Life.

Everyday. Every time. Everywhere. New tries and new tears arise.

All this comes with this journey. The Journey of life.

It comes with Twist & turns. Ups & downs. Try & cry.

But in the end, comes the joy. That brings hope. The hope.

That brings peace. The peace. That brings fulfillment.

And the bonding. And the stories of your Journey. Of my Journey. Of our Journey. The Journey of life.

Special thanks to all the awesome and amazing individuals that I met on the journey that produced this book. I know you are not thinking that I did it all by myself. Thank you Brooke-Sidney J. Habour, for editing this script, I appreciate your patience and diligence, God bless you. Desiree Lee for teaching me how to self publish, I love you lady continue to pass down the mustard seed. Mama Louise A O'Shields for making me realize the obvious… "I am a miracle"! I love you mama you are a miracle to us. Thank you Miss Katya Varbanova and the entire #peri10k family you guys made me see the best in me especially Michala Leyland, Jai Garcia, Nabisubi Musoke, Stefanie Rennert, Marlene Rennert,

Daniel Roberts, Kathryn Huber, Cyndi Po (Momma Po), Lauri Li, Collier Ma, Carolina Raeburn and Cordelia Gaffar. Special thanks to the members of #Afriscopetv community particularly Monique Hackett and Habiba kehinde for holding down the forth while I wrote, and also Princess Fumi Hancock; for introducing the #QuitYourJobin90Days challenge, Toni Henderson-Mayers, Janice Temple, Jumoke Fasoyinu, Fred Nonterah, Queenette Nwobodo, Nneka Irene, Esta Morenikeji, J Hamilton McCoy, Sara Holland, Ruth Zubairu, Olufunke Imarenezor and every other person in Afriscopetv, love, unity and togetherness. Thank you Maryjoy P Cinense for encouraging me to do my first scope. To my dearest one and only Mich and the kids, kudos for providing peace and tranquility that sustained this book. And finally, to all my friends and family that I have not mentioned here thank you for supporting and believing in me. Love you all.

About the Author

Nkechi Ajaeroh is an army reservist, stay-home military wife, who went from living an unfulfilling life to an extraordinary life, becoming amazon number 1 bestselling author with "Elevate Your Life With The Power of Positive Perception: What I Now Know For Sure"

Nkechi Ajaeroh's company Just Positude Co. LLC is a positive attitude company, which is determined to change the world through the power positive perception, attitude and action. Nkechi's lifetime goal and global brand goal is to inspire, motivate and empower men and women through positive action, helping them to desire and become more. She is determined to empower women, mothers, and military wives, down casted and discouraged individuals to step into their purpose and get to the next level.

Nkechi want to see people win and succeed, become their greatness and create an impact.

Nkechi Ajaeroh is active in non-profit sector; her non-profit initiative, GIVEE (Girls Initiative for Value Education and Empowerment) supports girls' education in Africa with the donation of $1.00 from every sold copy of this book.

She lives in Williamsburg, VA. USA.

Nkechi Ajaeroh's other Projects

Radio Show

Elevate Your Life with Kechi Radio Show. Every Tuesday 7.30pm-8.00pm CST with the All nations Radio. Please join her and learn how to become the champion of your greatness. #ElevateYourLifeWithKechi

Listen here: http://allnationsradio.net

Girls Initiative for Value Education and Empowerment (GIVEE)

GIVEE is Nkechi Ajaeroh's non-profit initiative dedicated to supporting girls' education in Africa, Nigeria to be precise.

As a result of the challenges facing the girl child especially in the area of education, Nkechi took it upon herself to donate $1.00 from each sold copy of her book ("Elevate Your Life with the Power of Positive Perception: What I Now Know For Sure") to benefit #GirlsEducation. Regrettably though, that donation is no way near her budget of this program, and she created a GOFUNDME campaign for this initiative

www.gofundme.com/supportgirls

Hopefully, with this kind of initiative, in near future, no girl child will be #leftbehind in Africa and other parts of the world. Currently, this initiative is sponsoring two girls for a whole school year of 2016-2017 in Abuja, Nigeria. Please join this movement and support this humble cause.

For more information and/or support please visit:

www.givee.justpositude.com

To donate please visit:

www.gofundme.com/supportgirls

www.ingramcontent.com/pod-product-compliance
Lightning Source LLC
Chambersburg PA
CBHW060021050426
42448CB00012B/2840